QUEEN VICT(

A Life From Beginning to End

Table of Contents

Introduction

The story of Queen Victoria's life is a difficult one to tell if only for its duration. Victoria lived for 81 years and was Queen of Great Britain and Ireland for 63 of those years, six decades during which the industry, economy, society and foreign policy of Great Britain changed dramatically. The world Victoria was born into was a very different one to that which she left behind, and her life story is an incredible journey from infant heir to matriarchal Queen and Empress.

Victoria lived two lives. One was the public life of a Queen, and later Empress, who was at the service of her subjects and responsible for representing her nation to the rest of the world. The other life was a private one as a loving wife and mother of nine children, dedicated to creating a happy and productive household. Victoria made a valiant attempt to incorporate the public and private spheres of her life in a way no other woman had before, but ultimately it was too big a task too far ahead of its time.

Victoria's childhood was not a happy one, and her middle years were dominated by the death of her husband Albert, a tragic loss she never fully recovered from. However, there was much joy in Victoria's life too, in the glamour and folly of her early years as Queen, in her dedication to her work as regent, and in her large, influential family.

Unusually, the story of Queen Victoria's life has been written in part by her own hand. Victoria wrote an estimated 2,500 words every day, kept a daily journal, and wrote constant letters to family and friends. Described at different points in her life as a spoiled child, a stubborn young Queen, a subservient wife, a cruel mother, a reclusive widow, a benevolent matriarch, a warrior Queen, and a principled sovereign, there are many sides to Queen Victoria. We can only hope to begin to understand a few of them here.

Chapter One

An Unsentimental Marriage

"I will be good!"

—Queen Victoria

The story of how Queen Victoria's mother and father met and married is not a romantic tale. Nor is the story of Victoria's conception - which could accurately be described as the result of a crisis of succession.

In the year 1817, King George III was on the throne. George was of the House of Hanover, the Royal dynasty that had ruled Britain since 1717 when it took over from the House of Stuart. In 1817 there was only one clear contender to take over the British throne on George's death, his granddaughter Princess Charlotte.

Despite the fact that George III fathered 15 children – nine sons and six daughters – his sons had produced just one suitable heir between them. The sinful situation of George III's seven sons (who lived into adulthood) was, before 1817, as follows:

The Prince Regent (George), who later became George IV, was locked into an unhappy marriage with Caroline of Brunswick. The pair had one child together, Princess Charlotte before they were formally separated. George enjoyed the company of a number of mistresses.

The Duke of York (Frederick), was married to Princess Frederica Charlotte of Prussia. The marriage was unhappy from the outset, and the couple had no children together.

The Duke of Clarence (William); Duke of Kent (Edward); Duke of Cumberland (Ernest) and Duke of Cambridge (Adolphus) were not expected to figure in the succession as they were George III's younger sons. Except the Duke of Cumberland, all of George III's adult sons were either married but estranged from their wives or unmarried and enjoying a bachelor's lifestyle.

However, in 1817 the only clear and legitimate heir to the British throne, Princess Charlotte, died in childbirth along with her child. This tragic event created a dynastic crisis that threw the entire royal family into action. The Hanoverian dynasty was unpopular with the public, who thought their days as powerful rulers were numbered. King George III famously suffered from mental illness and most of his sons lived a lifestyle the British public deemed excessive and immoral. The family knew that key to keeping the Hanoverian dynasty alive was to secure an heir.

The middle-aged Hanoverian Dukes, whom Victoria often referred to later as her "wicked uncles," immediately sought out new wives to give them a legitimate heir. The Duke of Kent was the winner of this unsentimental race up the aisle as in 1817 he promptly discarded his mistress of some twenty-seven years, Madame de Saint-Laurent, and rushed into an arranged marriage to Victoire of Saxe-Coburg.

This union was the result of a careful dynastic calculation that saw the political benefits of uniting the houses of Saxe-Coburg and Hanover. Victoire was the sister of Prince Leopold of Saxe-Coburg, the husband of Princess Charlotte. Leopold had recently lost both his wife and unborn child and any claim to the British throne along with it, and he hoped that by marrying his sister to the Duke of Kent he could still stage a Saxe-Coburg takeover of the British crown.

Chapter Two

Race to Produce an Heir

"Conceived, born and bred...to mount the summits of greatness."

—Edith Sitwell

Although the marriage between the Duke of Kent and Victoire of Saxe-Coburg may not have begun on the most romantic footing, the couple did appear to be a good match and Victoire soon became pregnant. On the 24th May 1819, Victoire gave birth at Kensington Palace to the child who would later be named Victoria. The childbirth was witnessed by the Archbishop of Canterbury and other political figures, as was the custom when succession was under scrutiny.

At her birth, Victoria was fifth in the line of succession to the British throne after her father, the Duke of Kent and his three older brothers, the Prince Regent, Duke of York, and Duke of Clarence, respectively. The Duke of York attempted to disguise his designs on the throne and never mentioned the succession question in relation with Victoria, but Edith Sitwell nonetheless described the bouncing baby as, "conceived, born and bred...to mount the summits of greatness."

The Prince Regent was much displeased by Victoria's birth and did not wish to see the offspring of his brother take to the British throne, even if it was many years after his own death. The Prince Regent expressed his displeasure at the naming ceremony of the new heir in a somewhat petty display. Vetoing the name Georgina, which he felt too closely resembled his own, and Charlotte, the name of his dead daughter, he settled on Alexandrina Victoria, a foreign-sounding name chosen with the intention of making Victoria appear unsuitable for the British throne.

In 1820, both Victoria's father the Duke of Kent and King George III died within six days of each other. Victoria was just eight months old at the time. The Prince Regent succeeded to the throne as King George VI, and Victoria's position shifted to third in line to the British throne after her uncles, the Duke of York and Duke of Clarence, neither of whom had children.

Thanks to financial support from her Uncle Leopold of Saxe-Coburg, Victoria was raised at Kensington Palace in England by her mother, the formidable Duchess of Kent. Despite the fact that Victoria was in fact three-quarters German, she was raised to speak English as her first language and always addressed as Your Royal Highness. By Victoria's own admission in letters written later in her life, she was a spoiled child raised by a suffocating but affectionate single mother. Happy and healthy and, in portraiture, cherubic, Victoria was often described as a willful child. Despite Victoria's sylvan surroundings, her life at Kensington Palace was one of confinement. Moreover, she often described her childhood as an unhappy one.

"I had a very unhappy life as a child…," Victoria wrote in a letter to her daughter Vicky in 1858. "Had no scope for my very violent feelings of affection – had no brothers or sisters to live with – never had a father – from my unfortunate circumstances was not on comfortable or at all intimate or confidential footing with my mother…and did not know what a happy domestic life was!"

From the age of 11, Victoria's life changed dramatically when Lord Conroy entered the scene. Victoire, Victoria's mother, had few friends in London and spoke very little English. Historians have noted a rise of xenophobia in the British popular culture of the early nineteenth century, and this intolerance coupled with King George IV's clear irritation at her daughter's very existence, left Victoire lonely and vulnerable.

Lord Conroy came into Victoria's life masquerading as some sort of protector, playing on her mother's vulnerability by unnerving her with conspiracy theories. It is unknown whether the Duchess and Lord Conroy had a sexual affair, but what is clear is that Conroy quickly became the major male influence in young Victoria's life. Together Conroy and the Duchess subjected Victoria what they later dubbed the "Kensington System" of education. Under this system, Victoria was completely cut off from her royal relatives and consumed by a rigorous educational programme that taught strict moral codes of behaviour alongside arithmetic and languages.

The Duchess's resolve to raise Victoria as a future monarch was not completely selfless. King George III was still on the throne but was in very poor health. The Duke of Clarence (William) was next in line to the throne, and should William die before Victoria reached her 18th birthday the Duchess wanted to assure that she would be appointed regent in her place. The Duchess was successful in achieving this ambitious aim, and the Regency Act received royal assent on 23rd December 1830. In the year 1831, at the age of fourteen, Victoria first learned the exact nature of her royal destiny thanks to a genealogical table slipped into one of her history books. Her response to learning that she was a clear and close heir to the British throne was to say simply, "I will be good."

It later became known that what Victoria endured under the direct tutelage of the Duchess and her accomplice Lord Conroy was nothing short of abuse. The Duchess was essentially Victoria's jailer. Victoria slept in the same room as her mother and was constantly watched by members of her house. It is said that she was not allowed to walk down stairs without having someone hold her hand. Victoria was raised in complete isolation from others her own age, and she later admitted to being bullied by her mother and Conroy, who taunted and insulted her all the way into adulthood.

Chapter Three

Finally an Adult and Finally a Queen

"I trust to God that my life may be spared for nine months longer, after which period, in the event of my death, no Regency would take place."

—King William IV

The aging King William IV was not ignorant of the designs the Duchess had on his throne, nor of the undesirable influence of Lord Conroy. The King expressed animosity time and time again towards the household at Kensington Palace sparing just one member – Victoria herself. On the 21st August 1836, the King hosted a dinner party at Windsor Castle in celebration of his seventy-fifth birthday. Victoria was in attendance, and the King laid out his feelings towards the household at Kensington with characteristic frankness, saying:

"I trust to God that my life may be spared for nine months longer, after which period, in the event of my death, no Regency would take place. I should then have the satisfaction of leaving the royal authority to the personal excise of that Young Lady, the Heiress Presumptive of the Crown, and not in the hands of a person now near me, who is surrounded by evil advisors and who is herself incompetent to act with propriety in the situation in which she would be placed."

There was now no real chance of the Duchess becoming regent; furious at this very public snub, the Duchess took her anger out on Victoria. King William was very ill, close to death in fact, as Victoria celebrated her eighteenth birthday on the 24th May 1837. Victoria's birthday was not as happy an occasion as it should have been, as a terrible row broke out between Victoria and her guardians. King William had offered Victoria an establishment of her own, a clear attempt to break the control the Duchess and Conroy had over her. The Duchess refused the king's offer without ever speaking of it to Victoria, and Conroy threatened Victoria in an attempt to coerce her into officially appointing him as her political advisor.

The traumatic nature of Victoria's relationship with her mother and Lord Conroy was to affect Victoria for the rest of her life. Many biographers have pointed to Victoria's stubbornness and bad temper as the result of enduring an isolated childhood with an overbearing mother. The facets of Victoria's personality that led some to criticize her are in some ways the very things that saved her. The Kensington System had made her strong-willed and independent, traits she would need in abundance to rule as Queen. As soon as she was able, Victoria stepped out of her mother's suffocating grip, banished Conroy, and determined to rule alone.

Queen Victoria's coronation took place on the 27th June 1838 at Westminster Abbey. Huge crowds of well-wishers gathered to see their new Queen, and Victoria enjoyed a period of immense popularity. Recently turned eighteen years old with blue eyes, long dark hair, and a fresh complexion, Victoria was everything the British public wanted in their Queen after the long line of elderly Hanoverian kings. Of the day Victoria wrote, "beyond everything, and I really cannot say how proud I feel to be the Queen of such a Nation."

Despite the Duchess and Conroy's careful tutelage of Victoria, she knew very little of the political position of a monarch. The only person to really have an influence on her decisions during the earliest days of her reign was her Uncle Leopold, who counselled her in letters, warning against making snap judgements and becoming emotionally involved in political matters. Victoria moved into Buckingham Palace immediately and took revenge on her mother by denying her the title of Queen Mother and banishing her to a remote part of the palace. Victoria's published letters contain a succinct reference to Victoria's attitude towards her mother at this time: "I had to remind her who I was."

Victoria bonded with her first Prime Minister, the prominent Whig Lord Melbourne, instantly; her relationship with this fifty-eight-year-old man would dramatically shape her future as Queen. Victoria enjoyed a long honeymoon period as Queen, finding much joy in her summer court at Windsor. She met with Lord Melbourne every day and during their long conversations, which often extended over an evening meal, he taught her much of what the Kensington System had failed to cover, including her Hanoverian descent, the state of British politics, and what exactly would be expected of her as Queen.

However, the relationship between Victoria and her Prime Minister Lord Melbourne was a little too close for comfort and created a conflict of interest for both. Early in her reign Victoria had posed the question of whether or not she should appoint a private secretary. In the past, monarchs who were unfit or unwilling to rule alone had appointed unofficial private secretaries, such King George III, who was mentally incapable. To appoint a private secretary would be to undermine her own position as Queen publicly, but in truth Victoria needed guidance. Rather than appointing a private secretary to the Queen, Lord Melbourne decided to do the job himself, advising her on appointments and drafting all of her official letters.

In 1832 a Reform Act went through Parliament. The act made a clear distinction between the power of the House of Lords and the power of the House of Commons. Executive authority over political matters now rested with the Cabinet members of the House of Commons, rendering the authority of the monarch negligible. Victoria was still able to influence politics, though, and in May 1839 when Melbourne failed to win a majority in the House of Commons, Victoria stepped in. Melbourne was forced to resign from his position, but the Queen rejected the winning Tory minister, Robert Peel. On Melbourne's advice, the Queen refused to dismiss her Whig ladies in waiting as Peel had requested, a scandal that came to be known as the "Bedchamber Crisis." Victoria's actions effectively blocked the formation of a new government, the last time a monarch was able to do this, and Melbourne and his Whigs returned to office.

Around the same time, a scandal from Victoria's court hit the headlines of the British press. At the centre of the scandal was Lady Flora Hastings, one of Victoria's ladies-in-waiting who had been under the orders of the Duchess when Victoria was a child. Victoria wrote to Lord Melbourne that she believed Lady Flora was with child and that the father was undoubtedly Lord Darnley. The gossip reached every level of Victoria's court and, eventually, to clear her name, Lady Flora submitted to a medical examination. It was proven she was not, in fact, pregnant but gravely ill; she died soon after, possibly of liver failure or some other disease that caused her abdomen to swell.

Lady Flora's family were horrified at how the Queen had treated their daughter, and when they received no form of apology, they sent letters to the newspapers for publication. The newspapers jumped at the chance to publish such a scandal, and the Duchess of Kent, still haunting the remote reaches of Buckingham Palace, jumped on the bandwagon and shared stories with the press of how badly Victoria had treated her. At this point in her reign, Victoria is said to have been as unpopular with the British public as George IV had been at the time of his divorce. How could the Queen win back the hearts and minds of her public?

Chapter Four

V&A

"He comes to take 'for better or worse', England's fat Queen and England's fatter purse."

— Popular mid-nineteenth century cartoon

Years before Victoria was crowned Queen of Great Britain, all of the great royal houses of Europe had designs on who should be her king. One such design came from Duchess Augusta, the matriarch of the Saxe-Coburg-Gotha dynasty and Prince Albert Saxe-Coburg-Gotha's grandmother. Although Prince Albert and Queen Victoria were first cousins, Albert was groomed for the sole purpose of becoming Victoria's husband and king.

Victoria was not ignorant of this plan and spent a number of months pondering over Albert's suitability as a husband and, indeed, her own suitability as a wife. For a time Victoria showed an unwillingness to marry at all, citing her own obstinate nature as ill-suited to the submissive role of wife. However, Albert swept her off her feet.

On the 10th October 1839, Victoria received Albert at Windsor Castle with no intention of marrying him. Albert, for his part, was also said to have no intentions of marrying Victoria, and was intending to break off the whole courtship on this visit. In her journal Victoria described the first time she laid eyes on nineteen-year-old Albert: "It was not without some emotion that I beheld Albert – who is beautiful." After just five days in Albert's company, Victoria decided that she would like very much to marry him after all. In an unprecedented move, Queen Victoria proposed to Albert herself. Victoria did not have to ask anyone's permission to do this, but out of loyalty, she did let Lord Melbourne know ahead of time.

The young couple spent four months together before their wedding, a heavenly time for them both. They spoke German together, the language Victoria had been forbidden from speaking as a child, and by all accounts seemed to be very much in love. However, in matters of the heart and crown, it is never quite that simple. Despite the fact that Albert's own position in German royalty was fairly minor (in Coburg he was "serene highness," the lowest grade of royalty) he had been raised to rule a kingdom and did not take to the less prestigious role of husband to the Queen with ease. From its earliest days, the marriage between Victoria and Albert was a battleground of power and precedence in both the political and domestic worlds, worlds that were completely separate for most women of the time, but worlds Victoria was forced to occupy at once.

In order to advance Albert's recognition in Britain, Victoria promoted him to the highest rank of Royal Highness and fought to have his allowance raised by Parliament. Victoria commissioned William Ross to paint a miniature portrait of Albert, which she wore on a bracelet, and called him her "Angel" Finally, Victoria was able to put her lonely and unhappy childhood behind her and embrace a new life with her beloved husband, but Albert had greater ambitions than being merely a husband to Victoria; he wanted to reign.

Victoria did not give in to Albert's demands readily, and the first few months of their marriage were marred by a series of struggles during which both husband and wife were forced to make concessions. Victoria allowed Albert to blot the ink on her letters, using him as a sort of assistant but preferred that he assisted her only in the bedroom and not in any official capacity. The British public found a great deal of amusement in this arrangement and number of cartoons circulated depicting Albert as some kind of gold-digging gigolo. One such cartoon read, "He comes to take 'for better or worse', England's fat Queen and England's fatter purse."

Victoria and Albert were married on the 10th February 1840 in the Royal Chapel of St James' Palace, London, a day Victoria described as the happiest of her life. Despite her newlywed status, Victoria was unwilling to sideline her responsibilities as queen. On Albert's suggestion that they take a long honeymoon, Victoria snapped, "You forget, my dearest Love, that I am the Sovereign, and that business can stop and wait for nothing."

On a visit in 1840, Victoria and Albert's uncle Leopold expressed his opinion that Albert "ought to be in business as in everything necessary to the Queen." Leopold told Victoria that Albert should be her walking dictionary of reference and should be called upon by her to answer any questions she may have about pretty much anything. Essentially, Leopold thought Albert should be Victoria's personal advisor. However, Victoria had been warned against taking on a personal advisor as, in the eyes of her court and Parliament, it amounted to an admission that she was not up to the task of ruling Britain. Victoria still refused to share any officialdom with Albert.

Chapter Five

Die Shattenseite
(The Shadow Side)

"There is great happiness and great blessedness in devoting oneself to another who is worthy of one's affection...still men are very selfish and the woman's devotion is always one of submission which makes our poor sex very unenviable."

—Queen Victoria

Victoria and Albert's marriage may have continued along this vein for many years, with frequent arguments over power and precedence, had it not been for Victoria's first pregnancy. Within weeks of their marriage, Victoria discovered that she was pregnant, and her emotional reaction to this discovery was clear-cut – she was absolutely furious. Albert immediately moved his writing table into Victoria's sitting room in Windsor and placed it alongside hers. As Victoria was pregnant, Albert was appointed regent in the event that she should die in childbirth and on the birth of their first child, Victoria, Albert was given the keys to the Cabinet boxes and unofficially appointed Her Majesty's Private Secretary.

It was at this time that Queen Victoria experienced the first attempt on her life. In 1840, an 18-year old man named Edward Oxford accosted Victoria while she was riding in a carriage with Albert. Oxford fired on the pregnant Queen twice but either missed, or his guns had no shot. The Queen was unharmed, and Oxford was immediately seized and later charged with treason. Oxford was acquitted on the grounds of insanity and saw out his days in a state mental institute. The only motivation Oxford ever gave for his assassination attempt was "notoriety." Victoria's apparent bravery and level-headedness in the face of her would-be assassin led to a definite upswing in her popularity with the public.

Victoria's opinion on pregnancy, childbirth, and child-rearing, at least in the early days of motherhood, was that it an unpleasant but unavoidable duty of marriage. In her letters, Victoria refers to her role as a mother as die Shattenseite, "the shadow side" of marriage, a reference perhaps to both her dread of it and the hidden, shadowy way in which it was handled. Each time Victoria became pregnant and was forced into confinement, into the secret world of motherhood where so much was deemed unspeakable, Albert moved a step closer to his goal of ruling Britain as Victoria's superior.

To speed up his attempt to make Victoria subservient to him, Albert isolated her from her two closest companions. Up until the day Albert came into her life, Lord Melbourne had been the most dominant male figure in Victoria's life and her closest friend. Melbourne had retired from his role as Prime Minister after suffering defeat at the 1841 election and frequently wrote letters to Victoria from his retirement. The letters were for the most part simply friendly notes with little mention of politics or royal matters, but nonetheless, Albert put a stop to them, effectively banning correspondence between Victoria and the former PM.

A more difficult relationship to break was that between Victoria and Baroness Lezhen, Victoria's former governess. Victoria put Baroness Lezhen in charge of her court and household, something Albert was very much against. In January 1842, Victoria had recently given birth to her second child Edward when her first child, Vicky became ill. Albert seized the opportunity to blame the child's sickness on Lezhen, accusing her of mismanaging the household and neglecting the child. A furious row ensued at which time Albert left the family home and refused to communicate with Victoria except through letters passed through a third party. In one of his letters, he said, "take the child away and do as you like, and if she dies you will have it on your conscience."

Eventually, Victoria capitulated and dismissed Baroness Lezhen, a woman who had been by her side since childhood. This marked a turning point in Victoria and Albert's relationship. From this point on Victoria became consumed by her loyalty to and love for Albert and agreed to submit to his wishes in all things. Victoria re-wrote her own history, destroying many of the letters she had written before her marriage to Albert, dismissing them as "mere amusement, flattery, excitement and mere politics." Everything that had come before Albert was meaningless; Victoria was now entering the most important stage of her life and was determined to succeed in her role a good wife and mother.

Following Lezhen's dismissal, Albert carried out a complete overhaul of the running of the palace. It did seem that the management of the Queen's household left a lot to be desired. In 1838 a young boy was discovered in the palace kitchens. He had been living there unobserved for the past 12 months, and in 1840 another young boy was discovered sleeping under a sofa in a room next door to the Queen's bedroom. Such lax security would not do, and the household, in general, was incredibly chaotic and wasteful. Albert appointed a Master of the Household, and wasteful expenditure was immediately cut. In contrast to Victoria's court during the early days of her reign, which was a joyful place, jokingly referred to as "Camelot," Albert's court was more somber. Albert was of the opinion that a royal court should set a moral example; he introduced strict etiquette and forbade any discussion of politics or gossip. Victoria's amusing social life became a distant memory.

By the time Victoria had her third child, Alice, born in 1843, Albert had begun to attend meetings with ministers and sat on a throne directly alongside hers in the House of Lords. Albert's new status may have quashed the tension between man and wife, but it had intensified the tension between man and state. By his own design, Albert was the natural head of the family, manager of the Queen's private affairs, private secretary, confidential political advisor and assistant, tutor of the royal children, and permanent minister. Albert could hardly be considered a minister if he was not accountable to Parliament and there were many layers to his power. As Albert saw it, he was King in all but name, and Victoria was now merely an ornamental Queen.

In 1845 Victoria and Albert moved to an isolated spot on the Isle of Wight where Albert bought a seaside home known as Osborne using the Queen's private funds. Victoria was thrilled to leave London, where she felt she and her family were under increasing scrutiny from the press. She loathed living at George IV's Pavilion in Brighton and complained that she was regularly mobbed in the streets. Victoria had also recently been subjected to two further assassination attempts while riding in her carriage at Constitution Hill. Both attempts left her unharmed but gave her ample ammunition to defend her seclusion from criticism. At Osborne, the Royal Family became completely separated from court life and led a quietly productive lifestyle, just as Albert had wanted.

In the first ten years of Victoria and Albert's marriage, Victoria gave birth to seven of her nine children. At this time women were encouraged to take a "lying-in" period of six weeks following each birth. Add these periods to seven nine-month periods of pregnancy and Queen Victoria spent seven of the ten years between 1840 and 1850 bringing her children into the world. This arrangement suited Albert perfectly. Albert was free to take on more and more responsibilities during the time his wife was otherwise engaged, and a large family was his idea of domestic bliss as well as an important tool in dynasty-building.

Victoria's view of motherhood was unsentimental, to say the least. Time and time again she reveals in her letters how unpleasant motherhood could be and how much she resented what pregnancy did to her body. Victoria considered the first two years of her marriage "utterly spoilt" by childbearing and referred to her babies as "little plants" that are "frightful when undressed." And yet, completely in thrall to Albert, emotionally, sexually, intellectually, Victoria was content to be his subservient wife and mother to his children. As a result of her marriage to Albert, Victoria's attitude to her crown changed completely. Women, she decided, were not meant to govern.

Chapter Six

The Hungry Forties and Albert's Great Exhibition

"Nobody who has paid any attention to the peculiar features of our present era will doubt for a moment that we are living at a period of most wonderful transition."

—Prince Albert of Saxe-Coburg and Gotha

In 1846 Victoria gave birth to her fifth child, Helena. As Victoria enjoyed her lying-in period, a time during which Albert is said to have read out loud to her every night, Britain's political landscape was in a state of upheaval. Secluded in their seaside idyll, the royal family were far from the disturbing events unfolding across their kingdom. Victoria recorded in her diary at this time, "Really when one is so happy and blessed in one's home life, as I am, Politics (provided my Country is safe) must take only 2nd place."

In 1848, Victoria and Albert purchased Balmoral Castle in Scotland. After visiting the house in September 1848, it was quickly decided that the house was too small for ever-increasing Royal family, and architects were commissioned to build a much larger house on the land. Work began in 1853 and was completed in 1856.

The 1840s, the decade during which Victoria had seven children, were referred to by many as the Hungry Forties. In Ireland the Great Famine, which lasted for seven years between 1845 and 1852, killed over 1 million people with a million more leaving Ireland in the hope of building a new life elsewhere. The people of rural Scotland were hit by the Highland Clearances, during which thousands of Scottish farmers were forced from their lands, and in England and Wales the new urban working class swelled to epic proportions, bringing the quality of life in Britain's industrial cities to terrible new lows. A class war was bubbling between poor, working men and the Parliament and aristocracy that excluded them from both having an influence on government and a share of Britain's economic prosperity.

Against this backdrop of civil unrest, Albert orchestrated the Great Exhibition of 1851. On the 1st of May 1851, Victoria drove with Albert in a procession of nine state carriages up to Paxton's Crystal Palace in Hyde Park. This event could be described as the high-point in Albert's relationship with the British public. An intelligent man, interested in science, industry and the arts, Albert's Great Exhibition was highly profitable. The money raised during this grand show of British creativity and industrial ingenuity was used to establish several museums in Kensington including the V&A, the old Science Museum, and the Natural History Museum. Over six million people attended the Great Exhibition, and the Queen herself visited three times. An incredible spectacle, the Great Exhibition was successful in its aim to show the world that Great Britain was an industrial leader and held the key to a better future for all.

However, the pomp of the Great Exhibition and the spike in popularity Albert experienced following its success was short-lived. In the winter of 1843, the press vilified Albert as an enemy of Great Britain, accusing him of meddling in foreign policy and promoting German interests. The Crimean War was just around the corner, and anti-Russian sentiment in Great Britain spilled over into anti-German sentiment, making Albert public enemy number one.

In response to this crisis, Albert took an even firmer stance on the power of the sovereign, stating his view that the monarch (by now he saw himself as the monarch, not Victoria) should exercise supreme authority. Albert firmly believed that the sovereign held power over and above Parliament, but he did follow a strict code of political neutrality, something no other ruler of Great Britain had thus far managed to do.

Albert understood that in order to have power he must have information, and he began running Buckingham Palace almost like his own Cabinet Office. Albert began to rearrange the letters held in his sacred Cabinet Boxes, making duplicates and devising an elaborate filing system to help him to access information with greater ease, but he may have underestimated the labor involved in this task. In the mid-nineteenth century the monarchy, and indeed Parliament, was run on letters and documents, and Albert was forced to work tirelessly to keep up with the endless copying and filing of papers.

Delegation was not an option, and Albert felt the responsibility of transcribing letters written by the Queen or keeping notes of meetings with ministers was a duty that he alone could perform. By now the Queen relied on Albert completely to draft her official correspondence and was even prompted by Albert in German when making conversation over dinner with guests.

In 1853, the Crimean War broke out between the Ottoman Empire and Russia. Britain joined the war almost immediately in support of the Ottomans. The main effect of the Crimean War on Victoria and Albert's household was that Albert worked even more feverishly than before, spending hours and hours each day on his administrative tasks. On September 10th 1855, Victoria received a telegram at Balmoral, advising her that the twelve-month siege of Sebastopol was over, and the Russians had been defeated. The Crimean War had come to an end, and victory for Great Britain was assured. Victoria reached out to her public during and following the Crimean War in a way she never had before, forcing the government to build better military hospitals and barracks, signing every officer's commission by hand, and giving every medal in person. The Crimean War was the only major conflict Great Britain fought in for the entirety of Victoria's 63-year reign.

Chapter Seven

The Madness of Queen Victoria?

"Really when one is so happy and blessed in one's home life, as I am, Politics (provided my Country is safe) must take only 2nd place."

—Queen Victoria

Biographers of Queen Victoria set themselves an incredibly difficult task: the task of getting inside the mind of the Queen. Victoria's disposition, her nerves and sulks and tantrums, and her famous stubbornness have been recorded in anecdotes by any number of people who came into contact with her. However, Victoria was also a great chronicler of her own life, keeping a journal for many years and writing hundreds upon hundreds of letters during her life, and she frequently recorded her struggles to contain her emotions.

From the earliest days of their marriage, Albert had set himself the task of moulding Victoria in his own image, to create a woman who was always patient, always calm, and always collected. Albert convinced Victoria that her essential character was deeply flawed as a result of her upbringing and that he would teach her the valuable lesson of self-control. He certainly taught her subservience, but to eradicate the stubbornness and irritability that had been a facet of Victoria's complex personality since she was a child was a much greater challenge.

There are many references to violent scenes and terrible rows between Albert and Victoria in her letters. As one might expect, Victoria was prone to tantrums and anxiety attacks more often when she was pregnant than when she was not. By the time Victoria gave birth to her ninth child at the age of thirty-seven, her outbursts had become frequent and hysterical. Albert had a habit of quietly walking away from Victoria when she made a scene, punishing her later with patronizing notes that criticized her behavior.

Victoria's personal physician Sir James Clark recorded that he feared for Victoria's sanity in 1863, and there were some who thought that Victoria had inherited the "madness" that had taken hold of George III, Victoria's grandfather. Contemporary historians do not agree on the nature of George III's mental illness. Some point to a metabolic disorder known as porphyria as the cause of George's insanity, while others have diagnosed him as Bipolar with manic episodes. Either way, it seems unlikely that Victoria genetically inherited George's malady, but it was clear that she was prone to anxiety attacks and had a violent temper.

The next few years were difficult ones for Victoria. Albert retreated from her, spending more and more time on the mountains of paperwork he had created himself. Victoria did not wish to become pregnant again, and it is possible that the marriage became chaste at this time, something Victoria clearly struggled with. For years Victoria had made mention of the glorious intimacy shared by husband and wife and the everlasting passion she had for her lover and now, still in her thirties, all that had come to an end.

Victoria had struggled to build close and supportive relationships with her children and was characterized as a controlling and harsh mother. Perhaps Albert's lifelong project of controlling Victoria had simply caused her to direct her anger and disappointment elsewhere – towards her children. Victoria seemed only to be happy when alone with Albert and admitted quite frankly that she did not enjoy the company of her children. "I find no especial pleasure or compensation in the company of the elder children," she said and was jealous of the time Albert spent with them, particularly with her eldest daughter, Vicky.

Vicky was a child prodigy, extremely intelligent and talented at a great many things, and it is possible that Victoria was intimidated by her. In 1855, Albert arranged a marriage between fourteen-year-old Vicky and Frederick William, heir apparent to the King of Prussia, a dynastic match he had been planning since her birth. Albert was thrilled by the marriage, but Victoria did not approve of child marriage and feared for Vicky's health should she be forced to conceive a child while still a child herself. Perhaps Victoria's jealousy of her eldest daughter stopped her from intervening, or perhaps she was at this stage unable to contradict her husband in any way, but

Victoria allowed the marriage; Vicky was sent away to live in Berlin.

As Victoria had feared, Vicky became pregnant by her new husband. On hearing about her daughter's pregnancy, Victoria immediately penned her a letter, outlining how upset she was at the "horrid news." As Victoria had suspected, the pregnancy was a dangerous one, and Vicky almost died in childbirth aged seventeen. Now that Vicky and her mother shared an experience unlike any other, that of motherhood, their relationship blossomed. Living in different countries but writing to each other twice a week, the mother and daughter became closer than they had ever been while living together.

By contrast, Victoria's relationship with her eldest son grew ever more strained. Victoria freely admitted that she had never felt any real connection with Albert, known to all as Bertie, and she could constantly be heard criticizing him, to his face and behind his back. As a child, Bertie had not responded well to the rigorous study regime his father had created for him, and after consulting with a team of phrenologists, who looked at the formation of Bertie's skull, Albert was diagnosed with sub-normal intelligence. Bertie's temper mimicked that of his mother. It is possible that Victoria saw all of the qualities she despised in herself in her eldest son and that her attacks on him were a reflection of her own feelings of inadequacy.

Little did Victoria know that she would soon need the support and love of all of her children, even poor Bertie, more than she could ever have dreamt she would.

Chapter Eight

The Widow at Windsor

"Oh! That boy – much as I pity I never can or shall look at him without a shudder."

—Queen Victoria

On the 14th December 1861, Prince Albert died aged just 42; a tragic end to Victoria's fairy tale marriage and an emotional trauma she would never recover from.

It's not known exactly what caused Albert's death. In the years preceding 1861 Albert had clearly been in poor health, suffering regular bouts of violent stomach upset. Pains, sickness, and diarrhea had gradually been joined by depression and insomnia with no clear diagnosis in sight. Biographers have suggested that Albert may have suffered from Crohn's disease or another ulcerative bowel condition. It is also possible that Albert had developed bowel cancer. In the winter of 1861 Albert took to his bed, too ill and exhausted to leave it. On finding a rash across Albert's stomach, his doctors diagnosed Typhoid fever and told Victoria that Albert would almost certainly recover, but Albert soon developed the pneumonia that would kill him.

Victoria would not allow an autopsy to be carried out on Albert, but doctors advised her that overwork, stress, and worry were the major causes of the illness that had killed him. Victoria took this information but jumped to her own conclusions placing blame for Albert's death on the shoulders of one person, Bertie. Weeks before Albert's death, Bertie had caused a scandal by losing his (alleged) virginity to a courtesan named Nellie Clifden while on military exercises in Ireland. He was nineteen years old. The news rocked Albert's moral world, and he immediately set off to meet Bertie at Cambridge and give him a piece of his mind. Albert was already seriously ill at his point, and on his journey to Cambridge he was caught in a rainstorm and soaked to the skin.

To Victoria's mind, the stress of the scandalous news, the worry over Bertie's future, and the strain of the rainy visit to Cambridge had killed Albert, and she saw no reason to contain her thoughts on the matter. Her open dislike of her eldest son turned to physical revulsion when she revealed, "Oh! That boy – much as I pity I never can or shall look at him without a shudder."

Victoria retreated into a mourning period so deep and dark that she was never able to return fully to life as a healthy, still-young woman. Although Victoria was determined to keep on top of Albert's life's work in documentation, she refused to appear in public at all. Victoria avoided living in London, sharing her time between Osborne and Balmoral, both homes that she and Albert had built together. In these homes Victoria kept Albert's rooms as shrines, insisting hot water and flowers be put in them every day and dined alone as any conversation or laughter upset her.

Victoria was completely incapacitated by Albert's death and constantly bemoaned her broken health and weight gain. It took until 1866 for Victoria to agree to open Parliament in person. She arrived without any of a Queen's finery, wearing a simple black gown with a white widow's cap, and draped her red velvet cape over Albert's throne, sitting empty but still adjacent to her own. Despite her servant's insistence that she was perfectly healthy and well, Victoria refused to return to any real for of public life for most of the rest of her life, a decision that had a lasting effect on the monarchy as a whole. Victoria's complete retreat from political life set the precedent for a constitutional monarchy as opposite to a working ruler. As a grieving woman who refused to fulfil her public duty, Victoria was under threat from those who wanted to force her into abdication in favor of her son.

Bertie, now referred to as the Prince of Wales, was mercilessly criticized by Victoria. She wrote that he was, "totally, totally unfit for ever becoming king," and forced him to be a "social sovereign." The Prince of Wales was to act as the face of the monarchy in London society, but he was not allowed access to any state papers or to fulfil any kind of public role.

In the years following Albert's death, Victoria's relationship with her other children grew just as strained as her relationship with Bertie, though in other ways. During their marriage, Albert was constantly urging Victoria to have less concern for her own feelings and more for those around her. Now that she was alone,

Victoria became more self-absorbed than ever, adding the burden of her grief to that of her now fatherless children.

Rumour has it that on the night of Albert's death Victoria snatched her youngest daughter, Beatrice, then aged four, from bed, and made her sleep in her dead father's place wrapped in his nightclothes. The mourning period that descended on the royal household was strict and lengthy. Victoria's younger children still at home became accustomed to dressing only in black and were banned from engaging in any activity deemed frivolous. Cheerfulness and laughter were deemed, by Victoria, to be disloyal to Albert's memory.

Alice, Victoria's third child, was eighteen when Albert died, and had nursed her father on his deathbed. Unable to mourn in her own way, Alice was forced into the role of comforter to her grieving mother. Victoria clung to her daughters after Albert's death and demanded their company in a way she never had while her husband was still alive. Alice's wedding in the summer of 1862 to the Prince Louis of Hesse-Darmstadt was a sombre affair and immediately following it Victoria begged her newly-wed daughter to stay in Britain with her. Alice's husband could not agree to such an arrangement, and Alice began a new life in Darmstadt.

When it came to her next two daughters' marriages, Victoria tried even harder to keep them on British soil. First Victoria arranged for her daughter Helena to marry Prince Christian of Schleswig-Holstein, a German prince with few redeeming qualities, on the condition that he came to live at Windsor. Next, she forced her daughter

Louise to marry Lord Lorne, heir to the Duke of Argyll but a commoner nonetheless. Victoria's older children were horrified and told their mother as much in an exchange of letters that caused a major rift in the family.

Victoria vowed to play no part in the marriage prospects of her younger sons, but did hand out a list of unmarried Protestant Princesses, urging her sons, "choose for yourself amongst them." Leopold, the son with whom Victoria had the more difficult relationship after Bertie, for once heeded her advice and duly fell in love and married Princess Helen of Waldeck and Pyrmont. Victoria's second eldest son, Alfred the Duke of Edinburgh, married Marie, daughter of the Tsar Alexander II, against his mother's wishes, but seemed to suffer none of the serious displeasure reserved for Bertie.

Victoria openly admitted that she did not want Beatrice, her younger daughter, to ever marry. She hoped that Beatrice would remain her constant and lifelong companion and Beatrice fulfilled this role, a prisoner in her mother's dull court until the age of twenty-seven when she fell in love with Prince Henry Battenberg. Victoria reacted to this development and her youngest daughter's intention to marry with unchecked rage and forced the prince to abandon his army career and live with her at Windsor. Victoria claimed to have abandoned Albert's project to forge alliances with the great dynasties of Europe through the marriages of his children, and yet all of Victoria's children, apart from Louise, made a dynastic match that would later earn Victoria the sobriquet The Grandmother of Europe.

Aside from Victoria's meddling, constant criticism and periods of neglect, Victoria caused a huge amount of discord between herself and her children in her relationship with a certain servant, Mr. John Brown. In 1866 Victoria was living alone at Balmoral and spending the majority of her time with forty-year-old Brown. The relationship between Victoria and Brown transcended what was usual between a Queen and her servant, and they grew to be intimate friends.

It is impossible to know just how intimate a relationship Victoria had with her faithful servant but, expectedly, gossip was soon rife that the widowed Queen was engaged in an illicit affair. The Queen's household called her "Mrs. Brown" behind her back, and the press had a field day, reporting on every tidbit of information emerging from court. For four months a year, Victoria escaped to her Highland retreat and allowed Brown to take liberties that would never be allowed at court in Windsor. Brown is said to have blocked contact from others, especially her children and ministers, while Victoria was at Balmoral, and his influence raised the suspicions of many.

In response to the gossip, Victoria commissioned a painting of herself entitled, Her Majesty at Osborne, 1866, depicting the Queen in mourning sitting astride a black pony led by a black-kilted Brown. Furious about the "ill-natured gossip" concerning her relationship with Brown, the Queen found another excuse to isolate herself from fashionable society. However, gossip continued and does continue to this day about the Queen and her servant, with claims that the relationship was very much sexual and may even have led to pregnancy.

Brown died in 1883, aged just fifty-six, as the result of a skin disease. Victoria had recently injured her leg and was recovering in bed. On hearing of Brown's death, Victoria lost the use of her legs completely for several months and described herself in letters as feeling "utterly crushed," writing in the third person, "The Queen feels that life for the second time is becoming most trying and sad to bear deprived of all she needs." Brown was memorialized for all time with the commission of a bronze statue engraved with words penned by Tennyson: "Friend more than Servant, Loyal, Truthful, Brave/Self less than Duty, even to the Grave." Victoria's relationship with Brown did little for her reputation with the British Public and drove an even deeper wedge between her and her children and now, aged forty-six, Victoria again found herself alone.

Chapter Nine

Victoria and her Counsellors

"Grief is the agony of an instant; the indulgence of grief the blunder of a life."

—Benjamin Disraeli

Throughout the late 1860s, throughout the 1870s and 1880s, the Queen became embroiled in complex relationships with her Prime Ministers, one of whom became her best friend and one of whom became her sworn enemy.

Benjamin Disraeli is a fascinating historical character. A writer of Jewish birth, Disraeli brought much-needed gallantry and excitement into Victoria's life when he became Prime Minister in 1868. Having previously served as Chancellor of the Exchequer in Lord Derby's Tory government between 1866 and 1868, Disraeli served as PM for just nine months but during that time managed to make a lasting impression on Victoria, who later referred to him as, "one of the kindest, truest and best friends and wisest counsellors I ever had."

Disraeli referred to Victoria as "the Faery," likening her to the Fairy Queen Titania and flattered her with long and affectionate letters outlining how deeply he relied on her advice. Through gentle coaxing, Disraeli was able to convince Victoria that she must reclaim her position in the political system and come out of hiding once and for all. The timing was key. Victoria had recently published her book, Leaves from the Journal of Our Life in the Highland, a selection of diary extracts from 1842 and 1868 that were carefully edited to convey domestic bliss at Balmoral. While Leaves became a best-seller and ingratiated Victoria with many of her subjects, grateful for a peek behind the scenes of royal life, the book was not without its detractors. A very vocal minority criticised the Queen's depiction of endless, luxurious leisure, citing a price tag of £385,000 a year (the Queen's annual civil list payment) paid for by the working people of Britain.

If Victoria was to enter the public arena in a triumphant display of her worthiness as a sovereign the time was now. Unfortunately, the only man it seemed was capable of coaxing Victoria back into the limelight was more popular with the Queen than he was with the British public and lasted just nine months in office. Disraeli was replaced by Lord Gladstone, a man Victoria would soon come to despise.

Gladstone was not a perfumed cavalier, accustomed to wooing Royals, as Disraeli was. Gladstone was a stern man of conviction and resolve with no time for the gentlemanly ways of times past. That said, Gladstone was a staunch royalist, with a deep reverence for the institution Victoria embodied and a determination to safeguard her position against calls to dissolve the monarchy. The issue between Gladstone and Victoria was a battle of personalities rather than a battle of ideas. Victoria came to loathe Gladstone's manner, theoretical and idealist, and in turn, Gladstone was appalled by Victoria's neglect of her duties.

The same year Gladstone came into power Victoria built her "Widow's House," the Glassalt Shiel. Described by Victoria as the only place in the world where she could have complete rest, the Widow's House was completely isolated. A cheerless concrete building two and a half miles from Balmoral, the Widow's House sent a clear message from Victoria to Gladstone: the Queen is not to be disturbed.

Ill-feeling towards Victoria and, by extension, the whole royal family, continued to intensify. The Prince of Wales was torn apart by the press for his involvement in a scandalous society divorce case in 1870. The same year, Victoria agreed to open Parliament, a decision that suspiciously coincided with Louise, her fourth daughter's engagement and Arthur, her third son's, attainment of majority. The government would mark both events with financial settlements, an arrangement that outraged Victoria's critics who littered the streets of London with an anonymous pamphlet entitled, What Does She Do With It? Finally, when Victoria departed for Balmoral before the end of Parliament, there was a public outcry. Even Victoria's children banded together and wrote her a letter urging her to take her place in public and quash the burgeoning revolution.

Victoria had cried wolf too many times, and no one believed that she was ill or unable to perform her duties. The trouble was that this time, Victoria was telling the truth - she really was gravely ill. It was around this time that Victoria's faithful highland servant John Brown died, and she lost the use of her legs. Victoria suffered an extreme case of gout and rheumatoid arthritis and developed a dangerous abscess on her arm. The Times published an apology and, thankfully, the letter written by Victoria's children was never sent.

During Victoria's convalescence, the rumblings of a revolution could be heard coming from the north of England. Up to now revolution in Britain had been resisted. In Europe, conservatism, liberalism, and socialism were battling it out, but politics in England remained fairly calm thanks to the constitutional arrangement. Even as the Second Empire of France collapsed in 1848, Victoria's Britain had stood firm, but now republicanism was gaining popularity, with a rally in Hyde Park that attracted large crowds. Surprisingly, the only person who was able to overthrow the Republican animosity Victoria had created for herself was her least favourite child: Bertie.

As fate would have it, Bertie came down with Typhoid fever, the same illness that had killed his father, Prince Albert. Bertie was nursed at Sandringham with his whole extended family around him and a number of high-profile doctors at his disposal, but his illness only intensified. On the 14th December, the tenth anniversary of the death of Prince Albert, Bertie's doctor diagnosed that he was "on the very verge of the grave." The public was aghast, and expressions of sympathy for the Queen and her family poured in. Against all the odds Bertie recovered and a national service of thanksgiving took place on the 27th

February 1872, attended by Victoria. The event took over the city of London with well-wishers hanging bunting and celebrating in the streets, and as Victoria made a rare appearance on the balcony of Buckingham Palace, waving happily to the adoring crowds, it seemed a full reconciliation between sovereign and subjects had taken place.

Chapter Ten

Long Live the Queen and Empress – Victoria's Final Years

"'Oh, Albert...'"

—Queen Victoria

Now that Victoria was, at last, enjoying an almost unanimous popularity with her subjects, she began to take more interest in life outside the walls of her own sitting room. In 1874, Victoria's favorite politician Benjamin Disraeli again became Prime Minister, and together they reinvigorated Victoria's image, ensuring that Britain's golden age of industry and empire would forever be associated with her name.

During the mid-nineteenth century, Britain became a world leader in industry and trade and used its wealth and power to expand its empire drastically. During Victoria's reign, the British Empire added Canada, Australia, India and parts of South East Asia to its lands, doubling in size. This period of aggressive expansion was only possible thanks to Victoria's children and the dynastic marriages they had made. Related by blood or marriage to the royal houses of Russia, Germany, Sweden, Denmark, Norway

Belgium and Greece, Victoria was able to avoid any serious confrontation over Britain's expansion overseas.

It wasn't until 1873 that Victoria expressed a desire to take on the title of Empress of India. The East India Trading Company had been forcing India to succumb to British rule since the 1750s. In a series of conquests that began in Bengal but later expanded to Afghanistan in the West and Myanmar in the East, the East India Trading Company had begun as a trading body but gradually became involved in politics, paving the way for British Imperialism. Following the suppression of the Indian mutiny, India came under the direct control of the British government in 1858.

Victoria's new determination to officially assume the title of "Empress" was met with serious opposition. Two recent Reform Acts had changed the way the British government worked for the better. Many believed the Royal Titles Act, which would give Victoria her new desired title, was a step backwards for political progress and smacked of imperialism. Imperial titles were associated with Russia, Napoleonic France, and Germany, aggressive nations where ordinary citizens came under the rule of a single, often despotic, ruler.

Victoria got her way, and the diverse population of India became the subjects of Queen Victoria of Great Britain and Empress of India. Victoria's new title was proclaimed at an event on the 1st January 1877 by Lord Lytton, Viceroy of India, and was as magnificent an affair as could be. Dripping in the exotic jewels of the Orient, including the Koh-I-Noor diamond of the Maharajas of

Lahore, Victoria commissioned a number of new family portraits, and a photograph of herself sat upon an ivory throne.

Victoria's fascination with the exotic nation she would never see but would rule over from afar may go some way in explaining her relationship with Abdul Karim, who was twenty-four years old when he entered Victoria's household. A khitmutgar, or male waiter, Karim was one of two Indian attendants sent to Victoria by a British governor in India in 1887. The Queen made Karim her Indian Secretary and spent much of her free time with him. It was said that Victoria treated Karim as a sort of exotic pet, and his influence on the Queen aggrieved both her household and family. Convinced that racism was behind her household's dislike of Karim, Victoria dug in her heels and treated him with even greater favor. While Victoria may have had a point, Karim was not at all what she thought he was, and it was later revealed that he lied about his past, stole from the Queen, and even leaked secrets about British policy to anti-British organizations in India.

Victoria's reinvigoration and increased interest in the affairs of her government coincided with a series of crises in the Balkans that grew into the Russo-Turkish war. Disraeli, still Britain's Prime Minister at this time, supported the Ottoman Empire against Russia and its invasion of Southeast Europe. From her throne, Victoria demanded that her government and military be bold. In a letter to her daughter Vicky, Victoria expressed her position: "You say you hope we shall keep out of the war and God knows I hope and pray and think we shall – as to fighting. But I am sure you would not wish Great Britain to eat humble pie to these horrible, deceitful, cruel Russians?"

However, both Victoria and Disraeli had miscalculated public opinion on Britain's involvement in the Russo-Turkish war. Gladstone re-emerged from retirement, voicing his opinions against Disraeli's government and by extension, Victoria. Disraeli found himself defeated at the polls of 1880, paving the way for Gladstone's return. Gladstone was in office between the years of 1880-1885, 1886 and 1892-1894, during which time the relationship between he and Victoria grew ever sourer. Victoria was incredibly vocal in her dislike for Gladstone and his policies. On the subject of foreign policy, she accused Gladstone of demonstrating liberal reluctance to maintain British prestige overseas. Eventually, Gladstone's government collapsed in 1886 without Victoria's help, over his plans to introduce Irish Home Rule.

1887 was an important year for the Queen, as she not only got rid of Gladstone and welcomed her friend Salisbury into office, she also celebrated her Golden Jubilee. Victoria's Golden Jubilee was a celebration of the Queen's mammoth fifty-year reign. For the very first time, commemorative stamps were created; people marched in the streets singing God Save the Queen; fireworks were set off in the shape of Victoria's face, and she was showered with gifts from all corners of her Empire. On the 21st June 1887, Victoria drove to Westminster Abbey with an escort of Indian cavalry surrounded by royal relations and well-wishers. The Jubilee celebrations were exactly what the public wanted and served to galvanize their new appreciation of the Queen, who had ruled over them for half a century. Victoria telegraphed a message to her 200 million worldwide subjects stating, "From my heart I thank my beloved people, May god bless them!"

It's a shame in a way that the celebration of her Golden Jubilee was not the last major event of Victoria's life. Instead, the outbreak of the Boer War in 1899 would dominate the final years of her reign. Now in her eighties, Victoria initially greeted the outbreak of war with bravado. She was all in favor, said her private secretary of "teaching Kruger (the Boer president) a sharp lesson." From a wheelchair, Victoria waved off troops, visibly moved to tears, and issued 100,000 soldiers with a commemorative tin of chocolate in December. Defeat was not an option for Victoria and yet as the months rolled by news of lost battles and high casualties caused her severe anxiety.

Victoria died of a cerebral haemorrhage on the 22nd January 1901 at Osborne House. She did not live to see the end of the Boer War or to celebrate Britain's victory. Victoria spent her final hours with her whole family, children, grandchildren, even great-grandchildren around her. Her last words were, "Oh, Albert…'" Victoria was buried with Albert, the husband she could not have loved any more, in the mausoleum she constructed for them both. Finally, after 39 years, husband and wife were reunited.

Conclusion

Queen Victoria lived for 81 years and ruled as the Queen of the United Kingdom of Great Britain and Ireland for 63 years and seven months. She had nine children with her husband Albert, seven of which were born in the first ten years of their marriage, and had 42 grandchildren, 34 of whom lived into adulthood. Victoria more than earned the nickname "the grandmother of Europe," and had an incredible influence on the politics of 19th century Europe thanks to her far-reaching dynasty.

It is difficult to overstate the mammoth changes that took place in Great Britain during Queen Victoria's reign. Victoria oversaw the gradual establishment of the modern constitutional monarchy, watched English politics evolve, and the British Empire expand to such a size that the sun could never set on it.

The image of a Queen must be more than mortal, and as a public figure, Queen Victoria is unrivalled in her magnificence. Queen Victoria represents the almighty British Empire, the industrialised powerhouse that was Victorian Britain and all of the glamour and refinement of the Royal family.

However, as a private person Victoria suffered much loss in her life and never got over the blow of losing her beloved husband, Prince Albert. Victoria mourned Albert's passing for the rest of her life and spent many years living joylessly in seclusion, never truly able to move on and live as a widow. Known for her caustic remarks and unsentimental view of childbearing and family life, Victoria had a difficult relationship with her nine children but managed in the end to reconcile their many differences.

The same can be said for Victoria's relationship with her numerous ministers, counsellors, servants and subjects, all 200 million of them. During her lengthy reign, Victoria's actions were criticized at times, and she endured brief spells of unpopularity, but in the end, she was celebrated as a national icon who gave her name to one of the most important and glorious eras in British history.

Printed in Great Britain
by Amazon